The Multiple Perceptions of Duplicity's Demise

The Multiple Perceptions
of Duplicity's Demise

JOE LOVETT

POEMS

LARKSPUR BOOKS

Joe Lovett

The Multiple Perceptions of Duplicity's Demise

Poems

Library of Congress Cataloging-in-Publication Data
Lovett, Joe
      The Multiple Perceptions of Duplicity's Demise
      Poems

ISBN-13: 978-0615696744
ISBN-10: 0615696740

Library of Congress Control Number   2012916780

Book design by Joe Lovett.
Cover painting, The Multiple Perceptions of Duplicity's Demise, oil on canvas, 43"x43", by Joe Lovett.
Cover photo by Farzin Montazersadgh.

Printed and bound in the United States of America.

10 9 8 7 6 5 4 3 2 1

for Nicole

Contents

ALSO BY JOE LOVETT

• November's Victim •

• • •

Available @ www.larkspurbooks.net

LARKSPUR BOOKS

Sharp

Sharp insolent walk,
with an heir, characteristic of
an assured child.
Pleased–
Smug–
Indifferent if you disagree.

———————●———————

Reduction

Sitting–
Blank–
A stare–
Gaze–
No!
We must get on to the next phase,
reduction gives us so much more.

Walking down the street,
eyed with disdain.
Shadows fail to follow.

Let's command an audience,
vacant and devoid of the next step,
we cherish trinkets and shun the very
freedom we seek to achieve–
I've seen two faces, an encounter so
bleak, with an unusual ease.
Remember ours?
A line–
A half measure–
Toxic encounters–
Scenarios are played.

Towers and Pedestals

Wait!
The sun is out, but not for you–
It's a grand one indeed–
Our towers and pedestals, secrets and
societies, clubs, cliques and things to
create inclusion,
The entrance out of reach–
The sun is out–
It's a grand one indeed.

———————●———————

Drip

Drip–
Drip–
Drip–
Drip–
Drip–
Drip–
Drip–
Drip–
Drip.

———————●———————

This Thing

This thing–
This being–
A meaning given to the barest of
specimen, emotion, or intellect.
The truest light gives guidance, not to be
dimmed by the bloated voice of pompousness.
This thing–
This being–
The truest of specimens.

Resolute orders regain–
This post-position of posterity has placed us
within the calm confines of clarity–
Which can neither fulfill, nor deny sanctimony.

———————●———————

Parsimonious in his teachings–
However, the mouth of improvidence
is open wide for enticement– wonder–
Thrust of device.

The Place of Ingested Treachery

This wry faced harridan calls upon
court jesters and sentries to hold the
place of ingested treachery.
Far from the spectre of insolent
servants, confined in squalor.

Ornament

Ornament–
Blemish–
Surveillance–
The teller of truths exposed footage bound
for its destination, no corners left unturned,
we are stillborn into diplomacy.

Fervency must dissolve all who disapprove,
our travels negate the static qualms
of childhood fears,
Perform now–
Lessen the rank–
Arguments, resolute.

The Embrace of Madness

As if my hands were in the embrace of madness,
one might assume or contemplate–
The pupil with her bumptious voice, and that
smirk of self entitlement.
Obsequious arrangements made in the back room
of required need.

———————●———————

Dive bars

Sleazy dive bars–
What's the attraction?
A warm stool out from the cold,
with no room for compromise–
The echo of establishment negates all soul.

Spare Time

In my spare time–
They do this–
That–
The other–
In my spare time–
They do what?
That.

———————●———————

There are many numbers
soft in slumber,
a gift given to us in secret,
with precision and clarity.

Sour Skin

The sweet smell of sour skin
blushed and spotted–
Positions of compromise sold the past–
Death made its direction, cutting holes
through the masses, abandoning us
with fortune.

Blue looks good on your tone–
And who is to say that a pendant
would not stand out.
Is that not the vehicle of interpretation?

Beautiful Mimic

The mood cannot be lightened–
I am a beautiful mimic–
Life corrupts with disappointment.

Grind of Guilt

In turned wood I see teeth,
malicious scenarios within the banks
of my own property, trying to inscribe
and capture the grind of guilt.

———————●———————

Cradled Faults

Yes, I too have cradled faults,
I too hold empty chambers–
Ego grasps us all–
Bottom knobs control slow speed
solutions, making use of left turns–
Tiny tools acquire.

Stations adopt replacement–
Explanations restore timid acceptance–
I guess–
I'm still–
Well–
You know–
What was discussed earlier today.

Our narrator told the story,
well received with attentive ears–
The morning sky revealed millionaires
that create collections, often incomplete.
The price must merge–
Inflate–
Classify.

———————•———————

He's looking to remind–
The past taken and enjoyed.
My great grand slave on the train,
posted, for all to see.

———————•———————

Shallow Joys

Surge through–
Pass with whim–
Allow shallow joys–
Prepare and grin.

Stacks of Shame

The experiment has perfected technique,
our avoidance keeps us at length.
Formidable opponent,
shed stacks of shame–
It doesn't have to be now, just
whenever you get a chance.

Blind Observations

Pieces fall–
Reduction–
Let's resume our conversation
of blind observations, and wilt under the
face of obscure existence.
Cramped–
jarred, and uneasy.

———————•———————

The Requirements of Desire

The requirements of desire have been met,
let all be seated–
Still–
Our crowd eager,
with many willing participants,
Pandering–
Plotting–
Hoping.

———————●———————

Pilgrimage

A pilgrimage of execrated action
was discovered, upon this accepted
transgression, pressure was applied.
The signal dropped–
Unable to connect.

Pain–
Pleasure–
One in the same–
Such behavior has found us in the
ridiculous face of refinement.

———————•———————

Use only under explosive circumstance,
with limited exposure to humanity.
It looks like a sounds grip stretched to the limit,
as I've lost the desire to smile.
Let's laugh and taunt at the expense, dressed in
plaid to impress–
Only to amuse.

A Flawed Dissection

Excretions–
Faith–
A flawed dissection–
Shall we gain or fail?
Is there no in between?
A place only to exist without judgement–
I guess not.

We were both alive with
myth's inspiration–
Perceptions of intelligence must insult.

The Founders of Excrement

Tasks–
Clicks–
Letters–
Get off of my path–
Jungles in deterioration–
The founders of excrement are
enjoyed by all who pass.

The observations of one who only sees the phallic connotations of cylindrical events, always shows their true nature.

———————●———————

Alter egos often become apoplectic,
not for what could have been, but
for what has already taken place.
Within the arms of achievement,
abandoned issues reside.

———————•———————

Shall I Pour Another

A drink–
Or two,
Or three,
Or four, with an old friend–
An epiphany always seems to reveal,
unsure behind curtains of sheer magnitude.
Shall I pour another?

———————●———————

Labels coded–
Colors vary unable to accept–
Gash–
Gnaw–
Embrace adoration from the inside, hidden
beneath layers of embarrassment, and
textures of substance.

———————●———————

Light blue sky, dark blue clouds,
Transitions between–
Like sunset.

———————●———————

A combination true and exposed for all to see–
captured honestly and sincere.

———————●———————

Maturity also has its doubts,
with this it concurs–
As a king–
taunting in it's nature,
guilty until presumed.

———————●———————

What it is– is the simplest form of logic,
a survival technique–
If only everyone would listen, realities relevance
would reveal, but the stubborn prevail as if it's
the norm–
Birth defects stain all walks of life.

———————●———————

Should I brand myself as something exotic?
Or just be? Without worry, fame or fortune–
There are no motives that are not ulterior, lets
compare ourselves to no one, and champion that
which lies within.

————————●————————

The Anger of My Ancestors

I hold the anger of my ancestors, they have been freed– but the past holds on, binding with no sympathy.

———————●———————

The Awakening of Mental Illness

Time falls before morning, and here it is–
The awakening of mental illness–
Production–
Motivation–
Indoctrination–
Innovation–
Consumption–
Deception.

———————●———————

The problem with you is that you're a
purest, and no one really cares–
Because its all about the bottom line–
All things must run their course.

Inherited Excuse

What will you procure with your inherited excuse?
A town?
A city?
A country?
A vacant land presumed, with unworthy occupants?

———————●———————

These are just questions that no one
has to answer.

———————•———————

COMPANY!!!
HALT!!!

———————●———————

Disingenuous laughter–
Vulgar renditions–
Deny everything.

How archaic are we really?
When tomorrow's advancements are
already a thing of the past–
Disarming–
Disheartening.

Will interruption forget?
What?
When?
Where?
I remember now–
Turn me to the side of production, strong
with sight– empty words of anger–
I work within linear despair–
My friends have passed.

Capability of minimal knowledge,
set back is temporary,
Stillness–
Pain–
Love will not understand–
Only through the cries of night,
do we devour our children.

———————●———————

We Wake With Lament

We wake with lament,
soiled in self reliance–
Such a thought, quick
now prodded and sore with tired
eyes of delusion–
We wear daily masks of society
in an attempt to resemble.

————●————

Notes of Reprimand

Oh how I do so miss those notes of
reprimand. A test run for the inevitable
as we lay in the carcass of existence–
What sort of data was she entering?

———————●———————

Stares and Loathing

Pushing past the stares and loathing,
our so called upper crust with
comparisons that pale.
Yes I do have a problem–
Yet I must confess, I am quite
comfortable, and our brief encounter
will hold no effect.

———————●———————

Harassment does not include dysfunction–
Protect the conduct that serves an
illegitimate purpose.
Reservations are at seven.

———————●———————

Totems, Monuments, Monoliths

Totems–
Monuments–
Monoliths–
Barks from the throat of the simpleminded
breeds plastic laughter contrived for acceptance–
The short fuse has been lit.

———•———

The maneuvers in which one
reveals, are telling in nature.
A knowledge of measures–
Scales–
Substantive justice, must embrace fictitious guilt–
Belligerent quotas face quick solutions.

———————•———————

Today will be no different,
our platitudinous surroundings fail to meet.
Inhabitants bore with execrable dialogue.

———————•———————

She was the most unlikely of candidates,
immersed within the practice of succinct
descriptiveness.
We sit solus–
Full of ardor.

———————•———————

Activity–
Points do not combine– expire–
Each separated by accumulation.

———————●———————

We Adorn Ourselves With Anguish

We adorn ourselves with anguish,
our tyrants polarized and denounced
without prescribed analysis.
The witness of condemnation has been silenced.

———————●———————

Within our new season
rests the dissolution of friendship.
Necessities outweight–
Ritual brings to us, a metamorphic process.

Shrines of Shame

Will death erase existence
or leave behind scars of human waste?
Placed within shrines of shame.

Flight Risk

Wild antidote for success placed
forbearance upon the driver,
Passenger–
Flight risk–
Bondsmen are equipped to retrieve.

Now and then they will appear
as if it were yesterday's dream,
a whisper of life imagined,
beyond truths and reflection.

Tones of harmony enliven–
Sounds of stillness brace us with calm–
Passion will grace our tastes.

———————●———————

The prognostications–
The savants–
The placed for function–
The spoon fed masses.

She was assailed–
despondency followed.

———————●———————

Flagrant Faces

For this we must apologize–
flagrant faces push past.
Unpolished, without recognition.

———●———

Islands employee immigrants of isolation.

———————•———————

Value perceived–
our emoluments accumulate dysfunction.

———————●———————

Strike Fast

Strike fast, wade through shallow streams
glistening within memory–
Retrace the steps of a boyhood dream–
Strike fast–
Time has been shared with offspring.

Side shows–
Streetcars bathed in simultaneous delight.
Our pachyderms pull captured patterns
destined for greatness.

———————•———————

Knowledge of wealth, staffs the minute
perception of perfection.
Macabre–
Resolute.

———————•———————

Thread bare on the periphery of
penurious confines, we toast to the
casual despondency which lay steadfast
upon our laps.

———————●———————

Savor the placid position,
our meals digest toward
facial expressions.

———————●———————

Shed Skin

Our cunning crop lords run seed
banks within the murk of deception,
with proclamations, claiming to be
champions of humanity–
Shed skin reveals.

———————•———————

Sleep now my lovely child–
Tuck soft, secure in slumber.

———●———

My past life has reawakened desolation–
enthralled with the potential of madness.

Spies and Satellites

Opinions–
Minions–
Spies and satellites–
Go ahead– speak your mind–
Have your say–
It only costs ten cents.

The History of Violence

One can succumb to the history of violence, and
proceed to write contiguous articles of such events.
Becoming products of the rewritten.

———————•———————

And now that the threshold has been
broken, our capacity must complete.
Morsels satisfy statistics of the flesh,
bounties are brought to us in the night.

———————•———————

Symbols

Symbols direct–
Symbols misguide–
Symbols are vessels of systematic control.

———•———

Peer Groups

The seedy–
The needy–
The greedy–
I've seen them all within the confines of peer
groups, with heads laid back in correspondence.

———————●———————

Recycled Revelations

Their innate propensity for the most
brutal of crimes will pawn one self
off as having an original thought.
Recycled revelations–
Please review them carefully,
before the show is cast.

———————•———————

Raucous Liaison

Our liaison celebrated ambulatory occasions.
Our elders were genuine–
Honest–
Inquisitive–
When I'm done, I will then finish yours.

———————•———————

Translucent Wound

Under the scope of interrogation he
danced around his own ressurection.
A translucent wound, wet and seeping,
so far removed from hierarchy.
Humanities existance shed plight–
Suffering.

Dark Spots

If there are any dark spots on the floor,
please do not hesitate to avoid them,
for life finds me in mourning, as it relates
to the human condition.

———————●———————

Chided by the hierarchy of hypocrisy.
I've received missives from psychopathic
societies that find inspiration within the
purview of perversion.

———————●———————

Diaphanous Flower

We've enacted idiocy for the sheer sake of it–
Diaphanous flower, please reflect the light, and
wilt under onerous eyes.

———————●———————

Joe Lovett, American artist, poet and social activist, for more information about Joe Lovett please visit www.nvokestudios.com

www.larkspurbooks.net